A~Z
Of Writers' Character Quirks

A~Z of Behaviours, Foibles, Habits, Mannerisms & Quirks
for Writers to Create Fictional Characters

Writers' Resource Series

Paula Wynne

Prado Press

London, United Kingdom

Free Book

Pimp My Fiction

Secrets of How to Write a Novel: Learn Writing Techniques from Successful Authors of Creative Writing Guides

Improve your writing. Transform your novel into a page- turning bestseller. Ensure your success as a novelist.

Pick up your free copy: http://eepurl.com/bC336f

Dedication

To aspiring novelists who want to create
vivid settings for their novels

"A man who can't bear to share his habits is a man who needs to quit them."
Stephen King, *The Dark Tower*

More Books by This Author

Also by Paula Wynne
Create a Successful Website
Pimp My Site

Writers' Resource Series
Pimp My Fiction
A~Z of Writers' Character Quirks

101 Writers' Scene Settings
Torcal Trilogy
The Grotto's Secret

Author Contact & Copyright

Copyright © 2016 by Paula Wynne
Paula Wynne/Prado Press
United Kingdom
www.paulawynne.com

Ordering information: Special discounts are available on quantity purchases. For details contact the author via paula@paulawynne.com

First published by Prado Press 2016
24 Caunter Road, Newbury, Berkshire, RG14 1QZ

A~Z of Writers' Character Quirks/ Paula Wynne -- 1st edition
First Published 2016 by Prado Press
ISBN-13: 978-1530622023
ISBN-10: 1530622026
Cover Art: Paula Wynne and Kent Wynne
Editor: Betsy Smith and Rosalind Brookman
Design: Slavisa Zivkovic

A CIP catalogue record for this book is available from the British Library.

Contents

Introduction

"Nothing so needs reforming as other people's habits."
Mark Twain

When a writer gets a character in their head, often that fictional person starts talking to them. I am known in my family to 'have voices in my head.' My husband calls my characters 'squatters' because they come and go, depending on which writing project I am currently working on. Some linger much longer, determined to get themselves heard.

As I continue on my writing journey I am constantly looking for writing resources to improve my writing. I started gathering a smorgasbord of writing guides to help me create believable characters that would jump out at my readers and tug at their collars, making them worry what happens to the characters throughout the story.

There are many excellent creative writing resource guides on creating characters, and some that even give character templates. I have listed the best ones in the first book in my Writers' Resource Series, *Pimp My Fiction.*

But even if a writer creates an archetype character, a fictional person from a star sign, or a hero or heroine from the enneagram types, we have to give them unique traits and characteristics to make them real and not a walking cardboard cutout.

There are many ways to do this, and taking a look at the chapters on character creation in *Pimp My Fiction* will give you loads of ideas. But another way to ensure your characters are like real people is to give them habits and quirks.

While I found lots of excellent writing books, I couldn't find a list of habits and quirks to help me enhance my characters. So I started watching people and making notes.

Like me, you will most likely get inspired to create character habits from watching people. It's easy enough to do when catching a bus or train, or sitting in a station.

I wouldn't want you to start stalking people, but watching them closely for a while, from behind a book or newspaper (the bigger and more discreet the better) will make you realise little things they do that could be added to your resource character list. Keep a notepad handy and jot down the things that amuse you or intrigue you the most.

Creating Character Habits

For my 'Creating Characters' file, I started making a list of things I noticed about people in many different situations of everyday life.

Many writers watch people to inspire ideas for creating fictional characters. Human habits and quirks are ideal to copy and use to create our heroes, villains and other minor characters.

I started asking friends about their habits and before long, it became an after dinner party topic. It's amazing how, after a few glasses of Rioja, friends open up and share things they like and don't like about people they meet (I have promised to keep all habits generic).

While riding London's underground I watched a girl twiddling with her hair while chatting on her phone. Now and then she used her phone as a mirror. On another occasion I spotted another young girl twirling her hair into a thin spiral and then sucking on it. Was she nervous, thinking about something that had happened between her and her boyfriend or parents? Or did she do it out of boredom?

I don't often catch buses, but when I did once in London, I saw a man waiting for the bus. Or rather, I heard him. He kept jangling the coins inside his pockets. After a while I turned to glare at him, but he didn't even realise he was doing it. Then, strangely enough, when he jumped on the bus, he didn't *even* have the right change!

Making Characters Unique

These movements and gestures we display make us unique from the person beside us. Like the man jingling his coins and then not having the right change, our habits and foibles can be so deep-rooted we don't even know we do them. Often it takes a partner, parent or sibling to point them out for us to notice what we are doing.

I know a lot of people who forget things. Me, for one. I used to have a sterling memory, but now I often find myself saying 'What's her name' or that 'thingy-ma-jig.' There are probably millions of people out there who do the same.

Lots of people have habits like drinking, smoking, gambling, sex addictions (I once worked with a guy once who spent all his spare time on porn sites; eventually the boss found out!), and even food addictions.

When I was promoting *Pimp My Fiction*, I noticed there are even people who are addicted to entering competitions!

I am often invited to speak at events, and catching the train up to London gives me the perfect opportunity to scrutinise the things people do. I notice things like men who read the newspaper back to front, sports section to front breaking news. Actually, I think most men do that. That's just one of the little habits they have.

A few years ago, on a plane to Cape Town to speak at their book fair, I had to endure the lady behind me cracking her knuckles all the way there. Phew. Long flight! I was sorely tempted to peek at her hands, imagining she had gnarled knuckles from all that bone crunching.

People Watcher

I enjoy watching people talk, and I have learnt that most people do so with their hands. A lot run their tongue along their lips or bite their lips or stick their tongue out when they're thinking about something or trying to make up their minds. Other facial expressions, such as someone flaring their nostrils, also go into my notepad. Or finger tapping. My worst aggravation is those people who call you 'Luv' when they don't even know you and give you a forced wink. Their habits and foibles are worth listing in case one day I want a character who does that.

When you observe your colleagues or friends or people in public places, use their habits and foibles in your stories. Why not? Just don't give your characters similar names!

Whatever you decide to use, do it to reveal their character or emotions (more on this in a moment). Don't overdo it and annoy your readers so much that they put your book down.

Talking of emotions, if you don't have a copy of *The Emotion Thesaurus* by Angela Ackerman and Becca Puglisi, do yourself a favour and get one. It is one of the best resources a writer can have. It lists all emotions and explains how to 'show' emotions and not tell your reader about the emotion. In *Pimp My Fiction* I have listed it as one of the best resource guides.

Rather than the character traits that Linda Edelstein wrote about, which cover personality types and possible traumas that cause people to carry a certain trait into their adulthood, I am talking about those silly little things we do, most of the time without knowing.

In *The Grotto's Secret* I used one of my own habits on one of my characters. And when I had beta readers give me their feedback, one of them even commented on the habit, and said she did the same thing so it endeared her to the character. Wow, what a lovely thing for a new novelist to hear!

So, in this book we are going to look at those weird and wonderful things people do. If you see something strange that you think only you did, you're wrong. Others do it too. Or could I have possibly spotted you doing it while I was train spotting?

Who knows?

Fire Player

Under 'F' I have a list for 'Fire Player.' Sucking or chewing on a match stick is fairly innocent, but playing with fire is extremely dangerous. Some of the items I have listed border on Pyromania, which is an impulse control disorder where individuals repeatedly start fires in order to relieve tension or for an instant thrill.

I know a pub manager who is always playing with matches and lighting them to see the match stick burn down to his fingers. I watched his strange habits over many months. For their Guy Fawkes display he had to be in charge of lighting everything, especially the kids' sparklers. Luckily, nothing went wrong at that event, but a couple of months later I witnessed his impulse to throw the discarded Christmas tree into the glowing embers of the fire where I was sipping on a hot chocolate and warming my toes, only to be tossed out by the fire fighters who came to put out the flames when the chimney caught fire!

This book is not about disorders, but I have listed several 'bad habits' that could veer into a disorder. If you want to read more about habits that become disorders, read *Writer's Guide to Character Traits* by Linda Edelstein, or Rachel Ballon's *Breathing Life into Your Characters*.

It was only when I wrote *Pimp My Fiction* that I realised my list of writing resources covered most topics on creating fictional people, but I still hadn't come across a book or dictionary showing people's habits and quirks.

Then it dawned on me that my list could help other writers. So, out came all the notebooks, scraps of paper and even a few coffee-stained torn off serviettes. Whereas for writing my novels I usually delve into that particular file-box and rummage around until I find something that could suit my character, I finally started typing up my observations.

Now at last, I too have a proper list!

Habits v Quirks

Which is which? The definitions are so similar, which makes it unclear and difficult to understand. But there are subtle differences between them.

Just What Are Quirks and Habits?

The dictionary definitions overlap and vary. The OED defines a habit as 'a settled or regular tendency or practice, especially one that is hard to give up / an automatic reaction to a specific situation,' and a quirk as 'a peculiar behavioural habit.'

The Cambridge dictionary defines a habit as 'something you do often and regularly, sometimes without knowing that you are doing it' and a quirk as 'an unusual trait or behaviour, or something that is strange and unexpected.'

But what exactly is the difference between Behaviours, Habits, Mannerisms and Quirks? Let's first look at the dictionary meaning for each:

Behaviour: Manner of acting or controlling yourself (behavioral attributes); the way a person behaves toward other people

Foible: a behavioral attribute that is distinctive and peculiar to an individual

Habit: an automatic pattern of behaviour in reaction to a specific situation; may be inherited or acquired through frequent repetition: 'she had a habit of twirling the ends of her hair.'

Idiosyncrasy: A behavior or way of thinking that is characteristic of a person, a slight glitch, mannerism; something unusual about the manner or style of something or someone

Mannerism: A behavioural attribute that is distinctive and peculiar to an individual

Quirk: an individual peculiarity of character; mannerism or foible

Habits

Habits are matters of daily routine, things your character has done so often that they've become automatic and would be extremely hard to change. Habits may be unique to your character or may be common in your character's community.

Looking both ways before crossing the street is a habit, though it's so useful and universal that it's likely to be unnoticeable (unless your character moves to the US from the UK and his neighbours notice that he looks right-left-right while they look left-right-left).

Checking that all the doors are locked before going to sleep may be a deliberate precaution in a dangerous place and time.

However, in a safe place and time it's likely to be a habit peculiar to your character, showing either that she once lived in a dangerous place or that she suffers from obsessive-compulsive tendencies.

Finishing other people's sentences is a not uncommon habit, but it may be highly noticeable and frustrating to people who aren't accustomed to it.

Quirks

Quirks are usually idiosyncratic (peculiar to the individual). And, they're likely to seem odd to the people who interact with your character.

Maybe your character cultivates quirks for effect. Maybe they've become habitual, or they're deeply rooted in his nature, and he can't readily change them.

Those who interact with your character probably won't be sure which sort of quirk they're dealing with. Repeating the last few words of the other person's sentence in a conversation may suggest involuntary mechanical and meaningless repetition of the words of another person, suspicion, or a strategy for getting time to craft a response.

Capping remarks with famous quotations may be a sign of an eager reader with a quickly-connecting mind, or of an ambitious person trying to demonstrate their knowledge.

Walking everywhere instead of driving or taking the Underground, even in bad weather, may suggest lack of money, or concern for the environment, or an extreme dedication to fitness, or simply a habit left over from a time when one of these forces was in effect.

You may find it easier to remember the difference between habits and quirks this way: Quirks are actions or behavioural personality traits that are deliberate. In contrast, habits are actions or traits that are automatic.

Bringing Characters to Life with Quirks and Habits

One of the hardest and most satisfying parts of writing is making your characters fully alive so your readers can recognise them, visualise them, believe in them and care about them.

Of course this requires careful use of story events, flashbacks, memories and dialogue. It's also helpful to flesh characters out with distinctive quirks and habits.

Quirks and habits serve several purposes in fiction. Here are a few major uses:

Identifying Characters

If your story includes a large cast of characters, assigning them distinctive quirks or habits may help your readers to remember them more vividly.

Charles Dickens makes use of this in his crowded novels: Mr. Micawber's unusually exuberant and redundant speech, and M. Rigaud's chronic scowl and tendency to sing snatches of La Marjolaine make them memorable—and also allow the reader to recognise Rigaud even when he's in disguise and using another name.

If your character is trying to go incognito, his quirks and habits may also betray him.

Defining Character

Habits and quirks can tell the reader something about the character's inherent traits and the environment in which your character was raised. Speech patterns and details of table manners may suggest something about your character's class background. Characteristic posture may suggest something about your character's level of confidence.

Of course, these are ambiguous and sometimes misleading clues. An upright, chin-up, arms-out posture may indicate a desperate attempt to put a good face on things. And, as the examples of habits and quirks given above demonstrate, most habits and quirks can be interpreted in several ways.

Revealing Tension

Many people, and many fictional characters, have certain quirks or habits which only appear, or which are accentuated, under stressful conditions. Speech impediments often get worse under stress. Hand-wringing, hair-pulling, glancing rapidly around the room and failing to finish sentences may all be signs of anxiety.

Creating Conflict

Sometimes conflicts in marriages, families, workplaces and churches arise from disagreements over matters of principle. Often they arise from petty irritations over habits. The character who thinks best in complete silence and the character who thinks best with music playing loudly are likely to make each other miserable if they have to work or study in the same space.

The character who is habitually early for everything will be perpetually exasperated with the character who habitually arrives fashionable late, particularly if they're ride-sharing. In a couple scenario, this is great subtle way to incite an argument.

This one defines my husband and me. He lives on the edge of time, whereas I prefer to be early for everything. Over time, and luckily with not too many spats, I realised when I needed to arrive early for an event or meeting it was best for me to arrange those, and then tell him we have to be there at an earlier time. He soon cottoned on to my little white lies and moaned about being too early! Thankfully, we now agree to disagree over what is early and what is late.

Habits and Quirk Shifts

So far we've been discussing habits and quirks as though they're fixed. But shifts in your character's quirks and habits can also give life and depth to your storytelling.

A shift may show the slipping of a mask, suggesting that your character isn't quite what she claims to be. See Character Creation in *Pimp My Fiction* for more on character 'masks.'

In Ngaio Marsh's mystery *Death in Ecstasy*, one of the suspects portrays himself as a rather clueless American businessman, and his speech is clogged with Americanisms, which grate on the Inspector's nerves. At one point in a police interview, he slips briefly and involuntarily into Australian slang, at which point the inspector starts inquiries, which end up revealing that character as a quite clever Australian confidence man.

A shift may also show an underlying transformation of character. Javert, the police-inspector in *Les Miserables* who has complete faith in the perfection of the law, typically walks upright with his hand tucked into the front of his coat. After a series of shocks force him to consider the possibility that the law may sometimes be unjust, we see him walking stooped forward with his hands clasped behind his back, his world falling apart around him.

In Dorothy Sayers' earlier mysteries, Lord Peter Wimsey's conversation is highly witty, elliptical, and strewn with slang and quotations, which are shown to be in part a defense for his shell-shocked nerves.

In her later mysteries, as his courtship of Harriet Vane helps to stabilise him and make him more willing to be vulnerable, his speech is more often clear and straightforward, though his wit and quotations never wholly desert him.

Adding Idiosyncratic Meat to Quirky Bones

With all this information under your belt, it's now time to start adding your habits and quirks to any new or existing characters in your writing projects.

To make it easier for writers to find a behaviour, habit, mannerism or quirk, I have grouped them all together in alphabetical order. So if you want your character to bite their nails, go to B for bite or N for nails.

Likewise, if your character likes to pick at their toes, you'll find their quirk under P for pick and T for toes. Of course you'll see repeats this way, but that's purely because we all search differently. You may go straight to nails to find foibles about nail biting, whereas another writer will go straight to find biting. This way at least you should find what you are looking for. Or browse through the alphabet to find inspiration to give your characters' weird quirks or habits.

You may prefer to have them sectioned by quirk or by habit (let me know if you do), however I think most writers would prefer poking around the alpha rather than fiddling between two different sections.

To ensure confidence for the people I have watched or friends who have shared their habits and quirks, I have been as general as possible. Using 'they' as a pronoun is not technically correct when referring to a habit that a person displays, unless of course there is more than one person doing that quirky thing. There are probably thousands, if not millions of people who have the same habits and possibly even similar or identical quirks. So I have gone with the 'they' and 'their' option.

Lastly, if you download the free Writers' Checklists (in *101 Writers' Scene Settings* and *Pimp My Fiction*) and stay on my mailing list you will be given the opportunity to get a free review copy of my next book, which is an Indie Author guide to book marketing with 100s of ways to promote your book.

Now, let's go explore some behaviour, foibles, habits, mannerisms and quirks for creating fictional characters!

A

Action

* Always gets in the middle of it
* Stands back instead of getting into the action

Addictions

* Aerosols
* Alcohol
* Chocolate / sweets – hiding them under pillow, hiding from friends and family
* Drugs
* Emails – always opens emails; can't start the day without checking emails and must end the day by checking emails
* Gambling
* Glue
* Mobile phone – checks phone every few minutes
* Online games
* Porn / porn sites
* Shopping sprees
* Sly behaviour used to hide addictions from others

Advice

* Always gives it out whether wanted or not

* Never takes advice from anyone because alreadyknows it all

Anger

* Always yells at people out of anger

Animals

* Has a weakness for rescuing stray animals

* Sleeps with the cat or dog when partner is away

Ants

* Sets ants on fire to watch them shrivel up and die

Anxiety

* Anxious around numbers, unable to do sums without calculator

* Becomes jittery and anxious after drinking too much caffeine

* Crosses and uncrosses legs when nervous

* Fails to finish sentences due to anxiety

* Glances rapidly around the room

* Hair pulling

* Hand wringing

Apologising

* Always says sorry, even when there's no need or it was somebody else's fault

Appointments

* Always arrives at least ten minutes early to any appointment
* Always arrives late
* Forgets appointments entirely

Arguments

* Always looking for an argument
* Agrees with viewpoints counter to their own, just to avoid an argument

Arms

* Always slides bracelets or bangles up and down arm
* Always taps someone's arm and says something like 'Hey, get a load of this.'
* Breaks out in sweat under arms for no apparent reason

Arrival

* Always early, makes sure to arrive for a meeting at least fifteen minutes early. If it's a speaking event, arrives an hour early ('fess up time, this is me!)
* Always late, this person lives on the edge of time, never gets stressed when late ('fess up time, this is my husband!)

Ass

* Scratches ass to the extent that it causes the trouser leg to ride up and down

B

Backs

* Always stands with their hands behind their back, sometimes in an 'at ease' position, even though they were never in the military
* Slaps people on the back

Balls

* Bounces balls against wall or on ground
* Practises keepy-up all the time
* Plays with balls (the testicular type) and fiddles or jostles them around in their hands, even in public; can often be doing this with their hands buried in their trousers
while having a conversation
* Pretends to kick a ball while standing in a group

Bangles & Bracelets

* Always jangles them
* Slides them up and down arm

Bathroom Habits

* Always in the tub, preventing others from using the bathroom
* Always takes a hot bath; not just hot, scorching hot. If the water is lukewarm or mildly hot, will not get in ('fess up time, this is me!)
* Particular about which bubble bath to use
* Drips water on the floor
* Fails to wash hands after using the toilet
* Leaves hair in the plughole
* Leaves the taps running
* Lights candles everywhere when having a bath
* Takes too many paper towels
* Washes hands excessively on bathroom trips

Bedtime Habits

* Always locks each bedroom and bathroom and other doors in their home at night before bed or before going out. Then hides the keys nearby, sometimes in gloves or old tea tins, very often forgetting where the keys are afterwards and unable to open certain doors of their home
* Unable to go to bed without a full glass of water or orange juice but seldom drinks any of it
* Checks that all the doors are locked before going to sleep
* Leaves the light on all night because scared of the dark

* Refuses to have anything on their bed that has touched the floor, such as luggage, shoes, pets' paws or even post that has been dropped on the mat

Behaviour

- **Annoying** (these could irritate another intimate character)
  * Clears throat excessively
  * Clicks or taps teeth with fingernail
  * Excessively uses initials or acronyms for common and uncommon phrases, never bothering to explain them
  * Engages in knuckle/neck cracking
  * Laughs at everything
  * Leaves tops off everything (bottles, toothpaste)
  * Licks cutlery after use
  * Never washes up, leaves plates piled up in kitchen
  * Plays air drums/guitar
  * Quotes movies/television shows all the time
  * Repeats the last few words of the other person's sentence in a conversation
  * Squeezes toothpaste from the middle
  * Slaps people on the back
  * Taps teeth with fingernail
  * Touches other people

- **Funny**
  * Constantly calls someone 'luv' and gives them a 'forced wink,' even if one does not know the person
  * Constantly carries a lucky charm
  * Constantly checks phone every few minutes

* Constantly coughs up phlegm, even when not sick

* Constantly cracks neck

* Constantly quotes favourite movies and usually identifies the movie that a quote came from

* Constantly uses a compact mirror to touch up makeup

- **Noisy**

    * Beatboxes

    * Clears throat

    * Clicks

    * Coughs

    * Farts

    * Hums

    * Sings

    * Taps

    * Uses cutlery to mimic drumming

    * Whistles

- **Obsessive**

    * Checks emails/texts

    * Cleans things

    * Lines things up on a desk or table

    * Washes hands

    * Washes dishes / kitchen counters

- **Repetitive**

    * Clears throat

    * Coughs

    * Hums/sings/whistles the same tune over and over

    * Sniffs

    * Stutters

- Unpleasant

  * Always misses the toilet/urinal and ends up with pee on the floor

  * Always sticks finger and thumb in eye sockets

  * Belches/burps

  * Constantly coughs up phlegm, even when not sick

  * Coughs without covering mouth

  * Farts

  * Farts in hand and 'catches' the smell, then with cupped hand goes to
    an unsuspecting victim and tells them to 'smell this'

  * Plays with balls (the testicular type) and fiddles or jostles them
    around in their hands, even in public; can often be doing this with
    their hands buried in their trousers while having a conversation

  * Picks at toes constantly until they are a mess

  * Scratches ass to the extent that it causes the trouser leg to ride up
    and down

  * Speaks with mouth full

Bending

  * Cracks toes by bending them right over until hearing them crack

  * Has several parts of body that are double-jointed and bend or flex in
    an unnatural or uncanny manner

Betting

  * Always eager to take them on

  * Constantly dares others

  * Takes stupid bets/dares for small amounts of money

Biting

  * Bites the flesh inside the lip

* Bites finger or toe nails

* Bites objects (erasers on pencils, pen tops, sleeves etc.)

* Bites on bottom lip

* Bites people's heads off (after quitting smoking/caffeine etc.)

* Nibbles instead of takes big bites

* Bites skin around fingernails

* Bites the top of a pen until mouth is full of ink

Blinds

* Has to have the blinds down when it gets dark

Blinking

* Excessively blinks, often when nervous, annoyed or embarrassed

* Rarely blinks, giving the impression of intensity

Blood

* Obsession with it

* Faints at the sight of it

* Writes in it

Body

* Suffers from abnormal dryness of the skin and always picks and scratches at their dry bits of skin

* Always fiddles with a particular part of the body

* Always on a quest to make themselves look ever more youthful

* Always sticks finger and thumb in eye sockets

* Always stands with their hands behind their back, sometimes in an 'at ease' position, even though they were never in the military

* So into nature that when they feel like being naked they take clothes off, no matter who is visiting

* Blows breath out through the mouth in exasperation
* Has noticeable body odour
* Clenches jaw
* Constantly rubs temples
* Constantly rubs tummy and saying 'Lovely jubbly'
* Cracks knuckles
* Cracks neck
* Cracks toes by bending them right over until hearing them crack
* Crosses and uncrosses legs or arms
* Excessively blinks, usually when nervous or annoyed or embarrassed
* Gets ill at the sight of blood
* Grinds teeth
* Has excessive dryness of the mouth and always licks lips to try and wet mouth, or chews gum to wet palate
* Has a twitch where they wiggle their nose, especially when telling a long story with lots of detail
* Has several parts of body that are double-jointed and bend or flex in an unnatural or uncanny manner
* Makes a colossal fuss whenever even the smallest spot appears
* Making noises with certain parts
* Opens mouth ridiculously wide when yawning
* Pees up walls, round the toilet bowl in circles
* Picks / bites /chews nails or skin (and eats it)
* Picks toes until they are a mess
* Pinches and pulls at any skin on any part of the body, especially at cheeks and chin
* Plays with balls (the testicular type) and fiddles or jostles them around in their hands, even in public; can often be doing this with their hands buried in their trousers while having a conversation

* Rolls eyes side to side or up and down, sometimes so far that only the whites of the eyes are visible

* Scratches ass to the extent that it causes the trouser leg to ride up and down

* Shrugs all the time

* Shrugs for no reason

* Slaps people on the back

* Speaks while chewing on the side of cheek

* Speaks in a zany manner with zany body language

* Stretches

*Suffers from bad zits, has scars on face

* Takes up too much room

* Suffers from tics (blinks, involuntary movements etc.)

* Twitches certain parts of the body for no apparent reason

* Exhibits unsavoury bodily habits
  (belches, breaks wind, picks nose etc.)

* Wriggles eyebrows

Books

* Always has nose stuck in one

* Bookshelves overflows with them

* Collects them

* Dusts them constantly

* Has to have all books on a table or desk in perfect order, none sticking out and all stacked up and square; if any become out of line or messed up, one squares them again

* Piles them high but never reads them

Boredom

* Constantly jiggles leg, often at a table, when bored, then when leg is exhausted moves to the other
* Crosses and uncrosses legs when bored
* Grinds teeth at night or in the day, when bored

Bother

* Always bothers about something
* Never bothers about anything
* Thinks any request is too much bother

Bottles

* Always leaves the lids off
* Chews lids of drink bottles

Bouncing

* Always moves, never stands still
* Bounces on balls of feet when nervous
* Bounces a ball off a wall or the ground

Breaking

* Breaks into song unexpectedly
* Breaks up tiny pieces of napkin and spits it into a straw. Secretly shoots it at unsuspecting people but quickly turns away so the 'shot' person doesn't know who did it
* Breaks out into sweat on brow, on nose or under arms for no apparent reason

Breathing

* Blows breath out through the mouth in exasperation

* Exaggeratedly
* Finds it really hard to cope with certain noises, such as over-exaggerated breathing
* Heavily
* Loudly
* Quickly
* Raspily

Bubble Gum

* Always has a packet
* Blows bubbles
* Chews with mouth open
* Sticks gum in unpleasant places
* Talks with a mouthful of gum

Bumping

* Bumps into people intentionally

Burning

(This kind of habit is extremely dangerous and some of the items below border on pyromania, so please see the note about this in my introduction)

* Watches a piece of paper burn all the way to the bottom
* Lights a match and lets it burn till it gets to the finger and then quickly blows it out
* Lights a match and waits for it to burn the tip of their finger before putting it out

C

Cabbages

* Sucks on cabbage cores

Candles

* Lights a candle and blows it out and relights it repeatedly

Caps

* Chews bottle caps

* Never seen without a baseball cap, a beanie or plaits

* Wears baseball cap back to front

Cars

* Always buckles up early or doesn't buckle up at all

* Argues with SatNav

* Car is filled with clutter, unable to find anything

* Drives badly

* Drives conscientiously

* Drives fast

* Drives slowly

* Shouts at other drivers from inside the car as if they can hear

Change

* Always makes sure to have change in pocket to give to beggars or the homeless
*Resists any type of change

Checks

* Always checks in calendar/diary before agreeing to anything
* Checks how somebody is throughout time together
* Checks hair whenever walking past a mirror
* Constantly checks emails
* Continually checks own image in mirrors
* Paranoid about make-up; constantly checks to see that it is perfect
* Secretly checks for dust in other people's houses

Chews

* Always chews on bits of wood
* Chews bottle caps
* Chews on pens or pencils
* Eats a sweet and chews it, doesn't suck it
* Chews gum (bubble, chewing gum)
* Hair
* Has excessive dryness of the mouth and always licking lips to try and wet mouth, or chews gum to wet palate
* Lips / inside of cheek
* Matchsticks
* Speaks while chewing on the side of cheek
* Straws
* Strongly dislikes the sound of chewing
* Toffees
* Toothpicks

Chewing Gum
* Always has a packet of gum with them
* Chews gum with mouth open
* Sticks gum in unpleasant places
* Talks with a mouthful of gum

Chocolate
* Binges on it
* Eats it constantly
* Hides how much is eaten from others
* Keeps it in the fridge so it's cold
* Sneaks back to the kitchen, time after time, to snack on more chocolate

Circles
* Eats the crust off a pizza, turning it around and around and eating in towards the middle until only a small inner circle is left and then savouring that last round bite
* Pees up the wall to see if they can do it in a straight line or around the bowl to make a circle

Cities
* Always knows the directions, even if only visiting a city for the first time
* Has no clue about directions, even after living in a city all one's life

Cleaning
* Always cleans home, office, desk, public toilet, etc. before using it
* Constantly cleans glasses / spectacles
* Dusts all the time
* Never cleans, happy to live in a pigsty

Clenching

* Clenches buttocks
* Clenches jaw

    (teeth have actually cracked and broken because of this. Most commonly, the face muscles really ache and headaches result)

Clothing

* Always dresses as a zombie for fancy dress parties
* Always wears lucky hat, socks, shirt or other article of clothing
* So into nature that when they feel like being naked they take clothes off, no matter who is visiting or where they are
* Clutches at a shirt
* Dresses for yoga and has all the equipment but never actually does it
* Has to have perfectly ironed clothes
* Never irons; clothes always full of wrinkles
* Never goes without a hat
* Often absentmindedly forgets to zip up
* Prefers zips to buttons on clothes
* Very particular about outfits

Clutter

* Has a very cluttered house
* Has a very cluttered mind, can't think straight
* Has a car so cluttered it's difficult to get in
* Hoards clutter

Coffee

* Always has a chilled ice coffee in hand
* A coffee snob

* Drinks too much caffeine, becomes jittery and anxious

* Never seen without a cup in hand

* Very particular about type of coffee ordered in cafés

Collecting

* Always looks for new items / trawls antique shops, vintage shops, auctions etc.

* Always talks about collection/geeky about it

* Books

* Comic book memorabilia

* Dolls

* Hats

* Junk mail

* Magazines

* Music – cassettes, CDs, vinyl

* Postcards

* Teapots

* Ties; even though owns 100s, still must collect more, despite never wearing any

Colours

* Matches the colours of stamps with the inked addresses, so the whole thing comes out quite a 'feast for the eye,' which always gets them a lot of praise from the letter recipients

* Never eats foods of certain colours

Complaining

* Always complains about everything

* Always switches lights off when leaving a room; complains if others do not do it

* Uncomfortable about complaining, even when something is really wrong
* Complains anonymously
* Complains loudly and embarrassingly in public

Computers

* Addicted to checking emails
* Addicted to checking text messages
* Always looks at phone, even when in company
* Always opens emails as they come in
* Always surfs the internet
* Coder
* Gamer
* Geeky PC collector, always hunts for parts
* Keeps computer/laptop running in the background at all times
* Never starts or ends the day without checking emails
* Plays gamer roles

Condiments

* Moves the salt and pepper pots around and around
* Lines them up obsessively on the table
* Steals salt and pepper pots from restaurants
* When dining out, always tidies up the table and resets the condiments

Cooking

* Collects recipe books, always tries new things
* Collects recipe books, never uses them
* An Enthusiastic cook, despite being terrible at it

Coughing

* Constantly coughs up phlegm, even when not sick
* Hackingly
* Nervously
* Smoker's cough

Crashing

* Plays with toothpicks, makes shapes with them or makes a pile and then crashes it

Crossing

* Always looks both ways before crossing the street
* Crosses and uncrosses legs when nervous, bored or agitated about something

Cups

* Always drinks from the same cup, flying into a rage if somebody else uses it
* Drinks only from plastic or paper cups and not able to stand the feel of glass in one's hand
* Refuses to throw favourite cup away, despite stains, chips, etc.

Curtains

* Has to have the curtains pulled when it gets dark
* Hides behind curtains to avoid answering the door

Cutlery

* Bangs on table to make a point
* Licks after use
* Points at people with them
* Uses them as drumsticks

D

Danger

* Faces danger head on, despite the risk
* Keen on dangerous sports
* Readily puts oneself in the way of danger without careful consideration

Dares

* Always eager to take them on
* Constantly dares others
* Takes stupid bets/dares for small amounts of money

Darkness

* Has to have the blinds down or curtains pulled when it gets dark
* Leaves the lights off and snoops around in the dark

Desks

* Has to have all papers or books on a desk in perfect order, no papers sticking out and all stacked up and square; if any become out of line or messed up, one squares them again
* Puts feet on a desk

Diets

* Always on one
* Always filling the fridge full of fat-free yoghurts as part of a never-ending diet
* Gives up dieting and binges on sweets
* Yo-yo dieting: weight constantly goes up and down

Dining

* When dining out, always tidies up the table and resets the condiments

Directions

* Always knows directions, even if visiting a city for the first time
* Never knows directions, even after living in a city all one's life

Dirt

* Has dirty fingernails or toenails
* Has mascara smudges under eyes from rubbing
* Places dirty dishes on top of each other in the sink

Dishes

* Allows dirty dishes to pile up and go unwashed for days
* Places dirty dishes on top of each other

Disliking

* Dislikes the sound of other people eating or drinking
* Has a huge dislike of people from a different country
* Strongly dislikes the sound of chewing, and hums a quiet song while eating
* Takes an instant dislike to people, things, places, etc.

Doodling & Drawing

* Always carries a pen or pencil to facilitate their habit of drawing random doodles on any piece of paper in front of them
* Always doodles on bits of paper
* Always has pen in hand
* Dots all i's with smiley faces /hearts
* Leaves little pictures everywhere

Doors

* Always locks doors before bed or before going out. Then hides the keys nearby, sometimes in gloves or old tea tins, very often forgets where the keys are afterwards and unable to open certain doors of their home
* Checks that all the doors are locked before going to sleep
* Leaves cubicle door open in public toilets
* Leaves the oven door open to give the kitchen heat
* Obsessed with checking that doors are locked/closed properly

Dragging

* Bags along the pavement
* Feet, even when happy

Dreams

* Day dreaming
* Explains them in detail to others
* Has a dream so vivid that they believe those things in their dreams actually happened

Drinking

* Addicted to alcohol, always drunk

* Always carries a bottle of water around

* Always needs to have ice in drink

* Always uses a straw

* Feels compelled to always wash a glass before drinking from it, even in a restaurant, so takes a trip to the loo before having a drink

* Bites people's heads off after quitting drinking coffee

* Constantly needs to drink or make a cup of tea

* Dislikes the sound of other people drinking

* Drinks only from plastic or paper cups and not able to stand the feel of glass in one's hand

* Drinks too much coffee

* Has to drink everything with a straw

* Knocks back iced drinks to experience 'brain freeze'

* Never drinks anything with ice in it

* Only able to drink out of a particular type of cup

* Slurps down drinks in public places to see what reaction comes from others around

* Unable to go to bed without a full glass of water or orange juice, but seldom drinks any of it

Drugs

* Addicted to drugs

* Criminal behaviour because of addiction

* Sniffs

Drumming

* Air drums to songs, real or imaginary

* Drums fingers against matching fingers, like playing a piano

* Drums fingers on the arm of a chair or on a table

Drying

 * Dries hands again and again

Dust

 * Always writes names or words in dust on furniture

 * Dusts all the time

 * Never dusts

 * Secretly checks for dust in other people's houses

E

Ears

* Always changes earrings
* Always cleans ears with a cotton bud
* Fiddles with earlobes or earrings
* Picks at ear hair
* Plays with holes in ears, even when not wearing earrings
* Pokes inside ears with a finger
* Tugs at ears or earrings

Earworms

* Driven mad by same song going through mind all the time
* Constantly sings/hums the same few chords/lyrics on a loop

Eating

* Always fills the fridge full of fat-free yoghurts as part of a never-ending diet
* Always licks their plate after each meal, or uses their fingers to mop up the leftover sauces; some may do this in public or in front of family while others may do this in secret
* Always on a diet

* Always munching on something
* Always nibbles, never takes big bites
* Eats a sweet and chews it, doesn't suck it
* Eats certain food in a particular way (peels off the cheese and then eats the toast, etc.)
* Eats food straight out of packets or jars
* Eats sweets and straightens out the wrappers or makes something from them
* Eats the crust off a pizza, turning it around and around and eating in towards the middle until only a small inner circle is left and then savouring that last round bite
* Eats the toppings off of the pizza, then the cheese, and saves the crust for last
* Eats too much after stopping smoking
* Eats yoghurts after every meal
* Finds it really hard to cope with certain noises, such as eating noises
* One food must not touch another on the plate, or they won't eat it
* Has food intolerances that cause illness (gluten, dairy, protein etc.)
* Hums a quiet song while eating
* Leaves one spoonful or forkful of each food item on plate and then eats that as the 'golden mouthful'
* Leaves best food item on plate to last and then eats that last
* Licks cutlery after use
* Nibbles instead of taking big bites
* Only eats in a clockwise pattern around plate, or vice versa
* Only eats food on plate in alphabetical order
* Only eats certain colours of some sweets, such as M&Ms

* Refuses to eat food of a certain colour, such as green food or yellow food

* Dislikes the sound of other people eating or drinking

* Strongly dislikes the sound of chewing, and hums a quiet song while eating

Eavesdropping

* Always listens in to other people's conversations

* Paranoid that others are listening in to conversations

* Eavesdrops in public, especially restaurants, and makes up stories about the relationships of the people around them

Electricity

* Saves electricity

* Leaves the lights off and snoops around in the dark

* Switches off plug sockets that have no plug inserted (UK plug sockets feature on/off switches in sockets)

* Switches the kettle off just before it boils

* Switches the toaster off just before toast is done

Emails

* Addicted to checking emails

* Always opens emails: can't start the day without checking emails, and must end the day by checking emails

* Opens emails as soon as they come in

Emotions

* Rubs hands together for any emotion

Excitement

*Yells when excited

Explaining

* Constantly feels the need to explain everything, even simple concepts

* Deliberately uses complicated examples or words, without explanation

Eyes

* Always makes eye contact with people

* Always sticks finger and thumb in eye sockets

* Excessively blinks, usually when nervous or annoyed or embarrassed

* Rolls the eyes to indicate disbelief or scorn; sometimes so far that only the whites of the eyes are visible

* Fiddles with eyebrows

* Fiddles with glasses

* Flutters eyelashes flirtatiously

* Lowers the eyes flirtatiously

* Lowers the eyes timidly

* Never makes eye contact with people

* Only able to make eye contact when really comfortable with somebody

* Pulls on eyebrows

* Raises eyebrows for no reason while speaking, either purposely or because of a twitch

* Rolls eyes side to side or up and down, sometimes so far that only the whites of the eyes are visible

* Rubs eyebrow hair back against the growth of hair

* Squints intensely at something due to poor eyesight

* Wriggles eyebrows

F

Face

* Always checks self in a tiny mirror or uses phone as a mirror to check lips or face
* Always dots i's with a smiley face or heart
* Points too close to somebody's face

Feet

* Always drags them when walking
* Always taps them on the floor
* Puts them up on the desk or table

Fiddles

* Body parts
* Buttons or zips on clothes
* Glasses or drink bottles
* Hair
* Hats
* Jewellery
* Moustaches
* Napkins/serviettes

* Spectacles/glasses

* Teeth

* Toothpicks

* Up nose

Fidgeting

* Always fidgets

* Unable to sit still at any time

Fingers

* Absentmindedly spins pen or pencil across the top of the thumb nail

* Always curls fingers in quotation marks

* Always plays with xylophone or running fingers across it to hear the sound

* Bites nails or flesh around them

* Chips away at nail varnish

* Clicks

* Constantly sticks finger in eye sockets

* Constantly twirls necklace between fingers

* Constantly wrings hands or particular fingers, sometimes behind back

* Cracks knuckles

* Drums fingers against matching fingers like playing a piano

* Drums fingers on the arm of a chair or on table

* Lights a match and lets it burn until it gets to the finger, and then quickly blows it out

* Lights a match and waits for it to burn the tip of the finger before putting it out

* Makes quotation marks when speaking

* Moves salt and pepper pots around and around

* Moves things around the table
* Paints nails to match outfit
* Picks at facial hair: eyebrows, eye lashes or moustache
* Picks fingernails
* Picks nose
* Plays with jewellery
* Runs a coin over knuckles
* Runs fingers along string of pearls
* Runs fingers through hair
* Slides the tip of index fingernail up and down along the side of the thumb beside it, especially if there is a snag or nail chip, and plays with it
* Snaps fingers
* Taps fingernail against teeth
* Turns ring round and round on fingers
* Twirls moustache round fingers
* Twists rings around fingers

Fire Play

(This kind of habit is extremely dangerous and some of the items below border on pyromania, so please see the note about this in my introduction)

* Constantly flicks a lighter on and off
* Constantly watches a flame on a lighter flickering
* Constantly watches a piece of paper burn all the way to the bottom
* Has to be the first and only person to light sparklers at Guy Fawkes
* Lights a candle and blows it out and relights it repeatedly
* Lights a match and lets it burn till it gets to the finger and then quickly blows it out

* Lights a match and pokes things with it
* Lights a match and waits for it to burn the tip of the finger before putting it out
* Lights matches for the fun of it
* Plays with matches but does not light them
* Sets ants on fire to watch them shrivel up and die
* Sets the Christmas tree alight in the fireplace and watches it go up in smoke
* Sucks or chews on a match stick

Flames

* Constantly watches a flame on a lighter flickering

Flirting

* Lowers the eyes flirtatiously
* Winks as a form of flirting

Flowers

* House always smells of fresh flowers

Food

* Adventurous, always keen to try new things
* Always licks their plate after each meal, or uses their fingers to mop up the leftover sauces; some may do this in public or in front of family while others may do this in secret
* Always munching on something
* Always on a diet
* Very fussy about what's eaten
* Intolerant to different types of food (dairy, gluten, protein etc.)
* Picks food out with toothpick or fingernail

* Sucks on cabbage cores
* Talks with a mouthful of food or gum
* Toys with food
* Unable to digest proteins correctly and gets very ill if too much protein-rich food is consumed

Forks

* Finds it really hard to cope with certain noises, such as knives and forks scraping on plates
* Licks knife and fork after meals
* Taps knife and fork like musical instruments

Fruit

* Sucks on a fruit pip and rolls it around in their mouth

Fun

* Lights matches for the fun of it
* Raises hand to wave at strangers for a chuckle
* Winks on purpose for fun

G

Gambling

* Addicted to gambling

Gas

*Saving gas:

- Leaves the oven door open to heat the kitchen
- Switches the oven off halfway through cooking

Glancing

* Constantly glances at watch
* Glances rapidly round the room anxiously

Glasses (Drinks)

* Always takes a full glass of water to bed but seldom drinks it
* Feels compelled to clean a glass before drinking from it
* Drinks only from plastic or paper cups, and unable to stand the feel of glass in one's hand
* Has a need to wash a glass before drinking from it, even in a restaurant, so must take a trip to the loo before having a drink

Glasses (Spectacles)

* Constantly cleans the lenses
* Fiddles with them whilst wearing them
* Looks over reading glasses when talking to somebody
* Plays with them
* Pushes them up and down nose
* Sucks the end of the arm
* Takes them off and twirls them round
* Uses one pair of glasses for watching cricket and another for watching rugby

Gloves

* Always locks doors before bed or before going out. Then hides the keys nearby, sometimes in gloves or old tea tins; very often forgets where the keys are afterwards and unable to open certain doors of their home

Gesturing

* Gestures a lot while speaking

Greeting

* Always offers a quick smile in greeting
* Casually greets somebody; barely raises an eyebrow
* Complicatedly greets a friend with an elaborate slap, shake and twist handshake
* Enthusiastically greets everybody with a hug
* Fist bumps
* Formally greets colleagues with a firm handshake
* Raises hand to wave at strangers for a chuckle

* Salutes anyone who passes

* Says 'hello' to everyone in the street

  (and spooks some people by doing this)

Grinding

* Grinds jaw (teeth have actually cracked and broken because of this. Most commonly, the face muscles really ache and headaches result)

* Grinds teeth at night or in the day, or when bored

Group

* Pretends to kick a ball while standing in a group

Guitar

* Plays air guitar to music, real or imaginary

* Always strums a guitar, particularly in company/at parties

Gum

* Always carries and chews gum

* Blows bubbles

* Chews with mouth open

* Smacks gum with an open mouth

* Sticks discarded gum in inappropriate places

* Talks with a mouthful of gum

Guy Fawkes

* Has to be the first and only person to light sparklers at Guy Fawkes

H

Hair

* Always fiddles with hair
* Constantly tries new hairstyles
* Constantly changes the colour of their hair
* Never seen without plaits
* Picks at ear hair
* Pulls hair in anxiety
* Pulls on hair until it hurts
* Rubs eyebrow hair back against the growth of hair
* Rubs hand over bald head or stubble hair as though in anticipation of finding more
* Runs fingers through hair
* Swipes hair to the side
* Tossing head to shake one's hair around
* Tosses hair back over shoulders
* Twirls hair into shapes and lets it spring back and then starts all over again
* Twizzles hair

Hands

* Always greets everyone with a handshake
* Always has a chilled iced coffee in hand
* Always stands with their hands behind their back, sometimes in an 'at ease' position, even though they were never in the military
* Always washes them
* Bites or chews fingernails or the skin around them
* Complicatedly greets a friend with an elaborate slap, shake and twist handshake
* Constantly taps fingers on things
* Dirty, particularly under the fingernails
* Suffers from dry skin on hands, always moisturising them
* Dries hands again and again
* Farts in hand and 'catches' the smell, then with cupped hand, goes to an unsuspecting victim and tells them to 'smell this'
* Fist bumps
* Formally greets colleagues with a firm handshake
* Gesticulates wildly while talking
* Has to always have something to fiddle with in a hand
* Raises hand to wave at strangers for a chuckle or for no apparent reason
* Rubs them together, either purposefully or as a nervous habit
* Rubs them together, for any reason or emotion
* Talks with hands
* When thinking, walks past a row of hedges, yanks off a green leaf and crumbles it up in their hand because they like the crunchy feeling as the leaf breaks up into little pieces. Smelling the fresh juice of the leaf as it gets on their hand makes them think of spring and connects them to nature

* Wrings them in sorrow or anxiety

* Writes with left hand, but does everything else right-handed

Hats

* Always wears a lucky hat

* Always fiddles with hat

* Never seen without a baseball cap or a beanie or plaits

* Never wears hats

* Wears baseball caps back to front

Heads

* Always talks to oneself in one's head

* Bites people's heads off after quitting smoking or drinking coffee

* Calculates the total of items put in a shopping cart and tallies it up in their head

* Constantly tosses the head

* Rubs hand over bald head or stubble hair as though in anticipation of finding more

* Sits on a beach and looks at the horizon to clear their head with a minimal, uncluttered view

* Tosses head to shake one's hair around

Head-Clearing

* Feels at one with nature, immersing in forests, woods etc.

* Finds peace when meditating through yoga

* Listens to peaceful music

* Listens to loud music and sings at the top of the voice

* Sits on the beach, staring at the sea, sea walks

Hedges

* When thinking, walks past a row of hedges, yanks off a green leaf and crumbles it up in their hand because they like the crunchy feeling as the leaf breaks up into little pieces. Smelling the fresh juice of the leaf as it gets on their hand makes them think of spring and connects them to nature

Hiding

* Addicted to chocolate; hides it from family and friends
* Addicted to sweets, hides them under pillow
* Always locks doors before bed or before going out. Then hides the keys nearby, sometimes in gloves or old tea tins; very often forgets where the keys are afterwards and unable to open certain doors of their home
* Hides behind curtains to avoid answering the door
* Hides from everybody through shyness

Hiking

* Keen on hiking

Hoards

* Clothes
* Junk mail
* Leaflets
* Magazines
* Newspapers
* Recipe books, or recipes from magazines
* Sports match programmes
* Takeaway boxes

House

* Agoraphobic, finds it hard to leave the house
* Allows dishes to pile up and go unwashed for days
* Always cleans and tidies home; keeps it spotless
* Always locks doors before bed or before going out. Then hides the keys nearby, sometimes in gloves or old tea tins; very often forgets where the keys are afterwards and unable to open certain doors of their home
* Has to have the blinds down or the curtains pulled when it gets dark
* House always smells of delicious cooking
* House always smells of fresh flowers
* House always smells of freshly baked bread
* House always smells of freshly brewed coffee
* Likes to yodel in the privacy of their own home
* Never cleans; has to step over rubbish or sweep it off the sofa to sit down
* Never leaves the house without a pen and paper
* Secretly checks other people's houses for dust

Hugging

* Always greets people with a hug

Humming

* Loudly
* Quietly while eating
* Repetitively
* Tunelessly
* Under breath

Hunting

　* Geeky PC collector, always hunts for computer parts

Hygiene

　* Allows dirty dishes to pile up and go unwashed for days

　* Constantly cleans glasses / spectacles

　* Never washes hands after using the bathroom

　* Obsessively washes hands

　* Washes hands at least three times after uses a public bathroom, even at one's friends' or family's home

I

Ice

* Always has a chilled iced coffee in hand

* Always needs to have ice in drink

* Knocks back iced drinks to experience 'brain freeze'

* Never drinks anything with ice in it

Ideas

* Submits to the ideas and suggestions of others without thinking of one's own needs

* Writes phrases and ideas on index cards to use them later in fiction

Illness

* Gets ill at the sight of blood

* Unable to digest proteins correctly and gets very ill if too much protein-rich food is consumed

Index

* Slides the tip of index fingernail up and down along the side of the thumb beside it

* Writes phrases and ideas on index cards to use them later in fiction

Insects

* Sets ants on fire to watch them shrivel up and die

Internet

* Always surfs the net

Interrupting

* Compulsively interrupts people telling stories to interject facts about the story that one only knows because one has been told the story before, not because one was involved with it

Ironing

* Always irons everything, even pants and handkerchiefs
* Never bothers with ironing clothes, always looks creased

Irritations

* Finds the noise of other people's eating annoying

J

Jargon

* Excessively uses jargon/acronyms/in-words without explanation

Jaw

* Clenches

  (teeth have actually cracked and broken because of this. Most commonly, the face muscles really ache and headaches result)

* Jerks jaw muscle

Jewellery

* Constantly turns necklace back to front
* Constantly twirls necklace between fingers
* Fiddles with pendant
* Jangles bangle/bracelet
* Slides bangle/bracelet up and down arm
* Slides necklace around neck
* Turns ring round and round on fingers

Jiggling

* Bottom lip, so there is a sucking sound coming from mouth
* Coins in pockets
* Legs, often at a table, when nervous or bored, then when leg is exhausted, moves to other leg
* Keys in hands or in pockets

Joints

* Cracks toes by bending them right over
* Has several parts of body that are double jointed and bend or flex in an unnatural manner

Juice

* Unable to go to bed without a full glass of orange juice, but seldom drinks any of it
* When thinking, walks past a row of hedges, yanks off a green leaf and crumbles it up in their hand because they like the crunchy feeling as the leaf breaks up into little pieces. Smelling the fresh juice of the leaf as it gets on their hand makes them think of spring and connects them to nature

K

Kettle

* Switches the kettle off just before it boils

Keys

* Always jiggles them in hand or pocket
* Always locks doors before bed or before going out. Then hides the keys nearby, sometimes in gloves or old tea tins; very often forgets where the keys are afterwards and unable to open certain doors of their home

Kicking

* Pretends to kick a ball while standing in a group

Kitchen

* Leaves the oven door open to give the kitchen heat

Knee

* Sways knee back and forth until it pops

Knives

* Finds it really hard to cope with certain noises, such as knives and forks scraping on plates

* Licks knife and fork after meals

* Taps knife and fork like musical instruments

Knowledge

* Always knows directions, even if visiting a city for the first time

* Always knows detailed info about people

* Constantly calls someone 'luv' and gives them a 'forced' wink, even if the person is unknown to them

* Unable to take advice from anyone because already knows it all

Knuckles

* Cracks knuckle joints

* Rolls a coin over them

L

Languages

    * Speaks in a foreign language to exclude somebody

    * Speaks in a foreign language to show off

Leaves

    * When thinking, walks past a row of hedges, yanks off a green leaf and crumbles it up in their hand because they like the crunchy feeling as the leaf breaks up into little pieces. Smelling the fresh juice of the leaf as it gets on their hand makes them think of spring and connects them to nature

Legs

    * Constantly jiggles, often at a table, when nervous or bored, then when leg is exhausted moves to other leg

    * Extends leg each time they sit down

    * Stretches out and takes up too much space around other people

    * Stretches out and deliberately gets feet caught up in other people's legs

    * Wears eye-catching trousers / tights

Letters

* Always sends handwritten letters with carefully chosen stamps. First, they buy philatelic editions from their local post office. Second, they make a point of properly 'theming' a letter to the person they are writing to; for instance, if they know the letter recipient likes cats or Star Wars or they have a special big birthday or they are Royalist, they will choose personality-matching stamps. Third, they match the colours of the stamp with the inked address, so the whole thing comes out quite a 'feast for the eye,' which always gets them a lot of praise from the letter recipients
* Kissing their letters when posting as a good luck symbol

Licking

* Has excessive dryness of the mouth and always licks lips to try and wet mouth, or chews gum to wet palate
* Licks their knife and fork after meals
* Licks their plate after each meal or uses their fingers to mop up the left-over sauces. Some may do this in public, or in front of family, while others do it in secret

Lids

* Chews lids of drink bottles
* Never closes the toothpaste lid after use

Lighters

* Constantly flicks a lighter on and off
* Constantly watches a flame on a lighter flickering

Lights

* Always switches lights off when leaving a room; complains if others do not do it
* Has to have the lights, radio and television on when home alone
* Leaves the lights off and snoops around in the dark
* Switches the light on and off twice before either entering or leaving the room

Lips

* Always applies lipstick
* Always checks self in tiny mirror or uses phone as a mirror to check lips
* Bites, chews or pulls on bottom lip
* Bites flesh inside lip
* Constantly licks lips
* Constantly runs top lip over bottom until raw
* Has excessive dryness of the mouth and always licks lips to try and wet mouth, or chews gum to wet palate
* Jiggles bottom lip so there is a sucking sound coming from mouth
* Wipes off lipstick and reapplies it

Lip gloss

* Always applies Chap Stick or lip gloss to lips
* Always carries lip gloss around; feels panicky without it

Lipstick

* Always applies lipstick
* Wipes off lipstick and reapplies it

Locks

* Always locks each bedroom and bathroom and other doors in their home at night before bed or before going out. Then hides the keys nearby, sometimes in gloves or old tea tins, very often forgets where the keys are afterwards and unable to open certain doors of their home

Loo

* Unable to go an hour without a cup of tea, even when travelling – but then must have constant trips to the loo
* Has a need to wash a glass before drinking from it, even in a restaurant, so must take a trip to the loo before having a drink
* Has to have double-thick loo paper or won't wee
* Has to have the loo roll facing down, not over the top
* Does not flush loo each time
* Pees around the bowl to make a circle
* Takes constant trips to the loo due to lots of tea drinking

Looking

* Always looks both ways before crossing the street
* Always tries to sneak a look at any x-rays on display when visiting a hospital
* Constantly looks at watch
* Looks up to the sky to avoid eye contact with someone
* Looks through eyelashes flirtatiously
* Looks through eyelashes shyly
* Regularly looks up at the sky to check the position of the sun or moon
* Sits on the beach and looks to the horizon to clear head

Losing Things

* Keys

* Money

* Purse

* Gets lost in thought while people are speaking and needs to ask them to repeat themselves

Lowering Eyes

* Flirtatiously

* Shyly

* Timidly

Lucky Charm

* Always carries one

Lying

* Makes up random lies about unimportant things for no reason

M

Mail

* Always weighs all small parcels and letters for either national or international post so they know what postage it requires upfront, and takes the parcel to the post office with airmail stickers, gift declaration and all stamps on letter or parcel

* Always sends handwritten letters with carefully chosen stamps. First, they buy philatelic editions from their local post office. Second, they make a point of properly 'theming' a letter to the person they are writes to; for instance, if they know the letter recipient likes cats or Star Wars or they have a special big birthday or they are Royalist, they will choose personality-matching stamps. Third, they match the colours of the stamp with the inked address, so the whole thing comes out quite a 'feast for the eye,' which always gets them a lot of praise from the letter recipients

Make-up

* Always applies or updates (lip stick, gloss, Chap Stick, mascara etc.)
* Constantly uses a compact mirror to touch up make-up
* Always uses phone as a mirror to check lips or face
* Leaves lipstick smears on glasses
* Has mascara smudges under eyes from rubbing

Matches

* Lights a match and lets it burn until it gets to the finger and then quickly blows it out
* Lights a match and pokes things with it
* Lights a match and waits for it to burn the tip of the finger before putting it out
* Lights matches for the fun of it
* Plays with matches but does not light them
* Sucks or chews on a match stick

Maths

* Able to keep running totals in head
* Anxious around numbers, unable to do sums without calculator
* Really good at mental arithmetic

Meetings

* Always arrives ten minutes early to any meeting or appointment
* Always arrives late to any meeting or appointment
* Regularly forgets scheduled meetings or appointments
* Stutters when meeting new people and then talks normally afterwards

Mimicry

* Mimicking an adult with a deep voice
* Mimicking others' voices or accents

Mirrors

* Always checks appearance
* Always checks self in tiny mirror or uses phone as a mirror to check lips or face
* Constantly uses a compact mirror to touch up make-up

Money

   * Always makes sure to have change in pocket to give to beggars or the homeless
   * Calculates the total of items put in a shopping cart and tallies it up in their head
   * Generous, always pays the bill or lends to friends
   * Has a thrifty nature, nearly to the point of obsessiveness or compulsiveness
   * Saves 20 pence pieces for no particular reason
   * Takes stupid bets/dares for small amounts of money
   * Thrifty, does not like to spend and knows where every penny goes
   * Unable to keep track of where money is going

Mood

   * Drags feet, even if in a good mood
   * Can have a high pitched voice, depending on mood
   * Can have a low, raspy voice depending on mood

Moon

   * Regularly looks up at the sky to check the position of the moon
   * Talks to the moon as if there really is a man in the moon

Moustaches

   * Forever changes styles
   * Has to style it exactly every time
   * Twirls the ends

Movies

   * Constantly quotes favourite movies and usually identifies the movie that a quote came from

* Obsessed with watching films about zombies
* Watches *The Sound of Music* constantly, just to practise yodelling along to 'The Lonely Goatherd'
* Watches re-runs of old films they have seen over and over

Mountaineering

* Keen on mountaineering
* Scared of mountains, won't go up them or even look at one

Mouth

* Bites the top of a pen until mouth is full of ink
* Blows breath out through the mouth in exasperation
* Chews with mouth open
* Coughs without covering mouth
* Jiggles bottom lip so there is a sucking sound coming from mouth
* Opens mouth ridiculously wide when yawning
* Smacks gum with an open mouth
* Speaks through the corner of mouth, either under stress or when telling lies
* Speaks with mouth full

Music

* Always plays with xylophone or runs fingers across it to hear the sound
* Likes to yodel in the privacy of their own home
* Taps a foot without any music being heard
* Taps knives and forks like musical instruments
* Thinks best with music on
* Watches *The Sound of Music* constantly, just to practise yodelling along to 'The Lonely Goatherd'

Moving

* Constantly jiggles leg, often at a table, when nervous or bored, then when leg is exhausted moves to other leg
* Moves salt and pepper pot around and around
* Moves things around the table

N

Nails

* Bites finger/toe nails
* Bites skin around fingernails
* Finds it really hard to cope with certain noises, such as nail biting
* Has dirty fingernails or toenails
* Lets nails grow extra long
* Paints fingernails to match outfit
* Paints toenails different colours to suit sandals/outfits
* Picks at skin around nailbed
* Picks fingernails
* Picks toenails
* Slides the tip of index fingernail up and down along the side of the thumb beside it, especially if there is a snag or nail chip, and plays with it
* Slides thumb nail along top or bottom row of teeth
* Spends hours each day painting toe nails

Names

* Forgets names and calls people 'What's-her-name' or 'Thingummy'
* Calls objects 'thingamajig' or 'whatchamacallit' or 'oojamaflip'
* Mixes up everybody's names

Napkins

* Always wears one in restaurants, even before the food has arrived
* Breaks up tiny pieces of napkin and spits them into a straw. Shoots them at unsuspecting people, but quickly turns away so the 'shot' person doesn't know who did it
* Calmly folds and unfolds
* Picks at a napkin/serviette and shreds it or folds it into shapes, or uses as a paper plane

Nature

* Always under canvas, camping
* Can communicate with animals
* Happiest when at one with nature
* House always smells of fresh flowers
* Keen on hiking, mountaineering, dangerous sports
* Lives in hut in forest/wood
* Touches and feels leaves, grass, etc. while outside
* Uses the sun to tell the time
* When thinking, walks past a row of hedges, yanks off a green leaf and crumbles it up in their hand because they like the crunchy feeling as the leaf breaks up into little pieces. Smelling the fresh juice of the leaf as it gets on their hand makes them think of spring and connects them to nature

Neck

* Constantly cracks neck

Necklace

* Constantly turns necklace back to front

* Constantly twirls necklace between fingers

* Loops and loops necklace

* Runs finger along string of pearls

Nerves

* Adopts silly or cartoon-like voices in times of nervousness or stress

* Always offers a quick smile in nervousness

* Bounces on balls of feet when nervous

* Coughs through nerves

* Excessively blinks, often when nervous, annoyed or embarrassed

* Jiggles legs, often at a table, when nervous; then when leg is exhausted, moves to the other leg

* Rubs hands together, either purposefully or as a nervous habit

* Shifts in seat

* Winks as a nervous tic

Newspapers

* Reads back to front

Nibbling

* Nibbles food instead of taking big bites

Noises

* Constantly makes annoying noises (clears throat, clicks, hums, knuckle cracks, whistles

* Finds it really hard to cope with certain noises, such as eating noises, nail biting and picking, knives and forks scraping

* Forever hears strange noises and goes to investigate

* Sways one knee back and forth until it pops

Nose

* A nose picker could do any one or all of the following:
* Picks nose
* Goes deep, as if they are mining, and then analyses what comes out on their finger
* Picks nose and eats what they find
* During a conversation picks nose as if it's completely natural, possibly not knowing they are even doing it
* Always rubs
* Always sniffs
* Has a twitch where they wiggle their nose, especially when telling a long story with lots of detail
* Pushes glasses up and down nose
* Taps or rubs nose
* Thumbs nose like a violin

Numbers

* Able to keep running totals in head
* Anxious around numbers; unable to do sums without calculator
* Really good at mental arithmetic

O

Obsessions

    * Animals: keeps them, rescues them, etc.

    * Bands: pop groups, boy bands

    * Celebrities

    * Cleaning: home, office, desk, public toilet before using, etc.

    * Curtains/blinds: closes them as soon as it gets dark

    * Germs: disease and contamination

    * Hair straighteners/curlers turned off

    * Thrifty by nature, nearly to the point of obsessiveness or compulsiveness

    * Has to have all papers or books on a table or desk in perfect order, no papers sticking out, and all stacked up and square; if any become out of line or messed up, one squares them again

    * Loses things

    * Makes sure that doors and windows are locked on leaving the house, at bedtime etc.

    * Makes sure the oven is turned off

    * Does not touch door handles, toilet flushes etc.

    * Objects: in correct place, orderly on desk or table

* People: a specific person or group of people; somebody known to them or a celebrity
* Superstitious: lucky numbers, objects, colours, doing things the same way, etc.
* Washes items before using them: crockery, cutlery, glassware etc.
* Washes hands

(Note: Some obsessions can become compulsive disorders, which this book doesn't cover. Read up on OCDs if you want your character to be anything like Jack Nicolson in As Good As It Gets where he washes his hands and throws away the soap, among other weird foibles like not stepping on a crack or joint in the pavement and has hundreds of locks on his door. He is a great example of a character with extraordinary quirks!)

Obstructing

* Finds ways to prevent things getting done
* Gets in the way physically
* Interrupts conversations with arguments

Oven

* Leaves the oven door open to give the kitchen heat
* Switches the oven off halfway through cooking

P

Paper

* Always doodles on bits of paper
* Constantly watches a piece of paper burn all the way to the bottom
* Has to have all papers on a table or desk in perfect order, no papers sticking out and all stacked up and square; if any become out of line or messed up, one squares them again
* Never leaves the house – or room – without a pen or paper
* Has to have double-thick loo paper or won't wee

Painting

* Always paints fingernails in matching colours to their outfits
* Spends hours each day painting toenails

Partner

* Sleeps with both the television and radio on and with the lights on, or with the cat or dog if the partner is not home

Pavement

* Walks in the middle of any aisle or pavement, forcing other people to move aside or around

Peanut Butter

* Eats peanut butter off the spoon
* Eats peanut butter straight out of the jar

Peeing

* Always misses the bowl and ends up with pee on the floor
* Pees up the wall to see if they can do it in a straight line, or around the bowl to make a circle

Pens & Pencils

* Absentmindedly spins pen or pencil across the top of the thumb nail
* Always carries one to facilitate their habit of drawing random doodles on any piece of paper in front of them
* Always taps a pen or pencil on the table
* Bites or chews on pens
* Bites the top of a pen until mouth is full of ink
* Chews the erasers off the top of pencils
* Doodles constantly on any bit of paper handy
* Never leaves the house – or the room – without a pen and paper
* Wears one behind the ear at all times

People

* Always finishes people's sentences
* Always greets people with a handshake
* Always greets people with a hug
* Always knows detailed info about people
* Always listens in to other people's conversations
* Always makes eye contact with people
* Always tries to recruit people to their religious or philosophical beliefs

* Always yells at people out of anger
* Bites people's heads off, often after giving up smoking, caffeine etc.
* Bumps into people intentionally
* Compulsively interrupts people telling stories to interject facts about the story that one only knows because one has been told the story before, not because one was involved with it
* Eavesdrops in public, especially restaurants, and makes up stories about the relationships of the people around them
* Finds the noise of other people eating annoying
* Forgets names and calls people 'What's-her-name' or 'Thingummy'
* Has a huge dislike of people from a different country
* Hides addictions and associated behaviours from people
* Imagines scenarios of what is happening to the people around them, for example, 'They may have had a huge argument; that's why they're not talking' or 'She's probably just had her hair dyed and he doesn't like it'
* Mixes up people's names
* Never makes eye contact with people
* Obsesses over a specific person or group of people, somebody known to them or a celebrity
* Often finishes other people's sentences
* People watching: spends time watching people going by and making up stories about their lives
* Points at people with cutlery
* Says 'hello' to everyone in the street (and spooks some people by doing this)
* Secretly checks other people's houses for dust
* Slaps people on the back

* Stretches out and takes up too much space around other people
* Stretches out and deliberately gets feet caught up in other people's legs
* Stutters when meeting new people, and then talks normally afterwards
* Takes an instant dislike to people
* Touches other people
* Walks in the middle of any aisle or pavement, forcing other people to move aside or around

Personal space

* Eavesdrops in public, especially restaurants, and makes up stories about the relationships of the people around them
* Encroaches into someone else's private space, so much so that the other person has to step back, which leads to the character stepping back into that person's space again. This can go on until the character has the other pinned up against the wall, not maliciously, just unknowingly
* Measures own personal space and ensures that others stay out of it

Pets

* Leaves the TV on during the day for the pets to have 'someone' home
* Sleeps with the cat or dog when partner is away

Philosophy

* Always tries to recruit other people to their philosophical beliefs

Phlegm

* Always clears throat with a phlegmy cough
* Constantly coughs up phlegm, even when not sick
* Coughs it into their palm and digs around in it to 'check it out'

Phone

* Always checks for text messages or missed calls
* Always uses phone as a mirror to check lips or face

Piano

* Drums fingers against matching fingers like playing a piano
* Plays an imaginary piano in the air or on other body parts

Picks

* Suffers from abnormal dryness of the skin and always picks and scratches at dry bits of skin
* Picks at a napkin/serviette and shreds it or folds it into shapes, or uses as a paper plane
* Picks at ear hair
* Picks at facial hair: eyebrows, eyelashes or moustache
* Picks at skin around nailbed
* Picks at teeth in public
* Picks / bites /chews nails or skin (and eats it)
* Picks fingernails
* Picks food out with toothpick or fingernail
* Picks nose
* Goes deep as if they are mining and then analysing what comes out on their finger
* Picks nose and eats what they find
* During a conversation, picks nose as if it is completely natural (possibly not knowing they are even doing it)
* Picks toenails

Pinching

* Pinches and pulls at any skin on any part of the body, especially at cheeks and chin

Pizza

* Eats the crust off a pizza, turning it around and around and eating in towards the middle until only a small inner circle is left and then savouring that last round bite
* Eats the toppings off of the pizza, then the cheese, and saves the crust for last

Playing

* Always plays with xylophone or runs fingers across it to hear the sound
* Plays air guitar / air drums
* Plays a tune with chopsticks
* Plays with balls (the testicular type) and fiddles or jostles them around in their hands, even in public; can often be doing this while having a conversation, with hands buried in their trousers
* Plays with glasses/spectacles, pushes them up and down nose, takes them off and twirls them or constantly cleans them
* Plays with holes in ears, even when not wearing earrings
* Plays with matches but does not light them
* Plays with toothpicks, makes shapes with them or makes a pile and crashes it
* Slides the tip of index fingernail up and down along the side of the thumb beside it, especially if there is a snag or nail chip, and plays with it

Pockets

  * Always has change in pockets to give to Big Issue sellers or
    the homeless
  * Always jiggles coins in pocket
  * Always jiggles keys in pocket
  * Always walks with hands in pockets

Pointing

  * Points too close to somebody's face

Poking

  * Lights a match and pokes things with it
  * Pokes about in ears

Porn

  * Has an addiction to porn
  * Hides behaviour around porn habit
  * Unable to have 'normal' sexual relationship due to porn habit

Public

  * Always licks their plate after each meal or uses their finger to mop
    up the left-over sauces; some may do this public, or in front of
    family, while others do it in secret
  * Always vocal in public, has to speak the loudest to keep the attention
  * Chews on a toothpick, a straw or a chopstick, often in public
  * Eavesdrops in public, especially restaurants, and makes up stories
    about the relationships of the people around them
  * Plays with balls (the testicular type) and fiddles or jostles them
    around in their hands, even in public; can often be doing this with
    their hands buried in their trousers while having a conversation

* Picks at teeth in public
* Slurps down drinks in public places to see what reaction comes from others around
* Washes hands at least three times after using a public bathroom

Pulling

* Pulls on bottom lip
* Pulls on chin
* Pulls on eyebrows
* Pulls on hair due to anxiety
* Pulls on hair until it hurts
* Pulls on skin on any part of the body

Putting

* Puts feet on a desk or table
* Readily puts oneself in the way of danger without careful consideration

Q

Quarrelsome

* Always looks for an argument
* Will agree with viewpoints counter to their own, just to avoid an argument

Questions

* Avoids eye contact – before answering question, looks up to sky

Quitting

* Bites people's heads off after quitting smoking or drinking caffeinated coffee

Quotation Marks

* Always curls fingers in quotation marks

Quotes

* Constantly quotes favourite movies and usually identifies the movie that a quote came from

R

Radio

* Always has to sleep with the radio on
* Changes radio stations after every song

Reading

* Falls asleep reading in bed / on public transport
* Never seen without a book in hand
* Reads the newspaper back to front
* Walks into things while reading

Relationships

* Always touches/fiddles with object of affection
* Close to family
* Constantly talks to/about object of affection
* Loner, has no friends/family
* Never goes anywhere without friend(s)
* Doesn't need friends/works better alone
* Stares dreamily at object of affection

Religion

* Always tries to recruit other people to their religious beliefs

Repeating

* Repeats the last few words of the other person's sentence in
  a conversation

Restaurants

* Compelled to wash a glass before drinking from it, even in a
  restaurant, so must take a trip to the loo before having a drink
* Eavesdrops in public, especially restaurants, and makes up stories
  about the relationships of the people around them
* Steals salt and pepper pots from restaurants

Rings

* Twists rings around fingers

Risk taking

* Considers all risks before acting
* Constantly assesses others' risky behaviour
* Faces danger head on, despite the risk
* Rushes in, never considers the risk

Rubbing

* Constantly rubs temples
* Constantly rubs tummy and says 'lovely jubbly'
* Rubs eyebrow hair back against the growth of hair
* Rubs hand over bald head or stubble hair as though in anticipation
  of finds more
* Rubs hands together for any reason or emotion
* Rubs nose, thumbing it like a violin

S

Salt and pepper

* Moves salt and pepper pot around and around

* Steals salt and pepper pots from restaurants

Saluting

* Salutes anyone who passes

Saving

* Eats the toppings off of the pizza, then the cheese, and saves the crust for last

* Saves 20 pence pieces for no particular reason

Scarf

* Only wears a scarf if they belong to the organisation it represents

Scenarios

* Imagines scenarios of what is happening to the people around them; for example, 'They may have had a huge argument, that's why they're not talking' or 'She's probably just had her hair dyed and he doesn't like it'

* Inventing plot scenarios from part personal experience and part make believe for futuristic tales

Scraping

* Finds it really hard to cope with certain noises, such as knives and forks scraping on plates
* Scrapes at fingernail polish

Scratching

* Suffers from abnormal dryness of the skin and always picks and scratches at dry bits of skin
* Scratches ass to the extent that it causes the trouser leg to ride up and down

Serviettes

* Always wears one in restaurants, even before the food has arrived
* Breaks up tiny pieces of napkin, spits them into a straw and shoots them at unsuspecting people, but quickly turns away so the 'shot' person doesn't know who did it
* Calmly folds and unfolds them
* Picks at a napkin/serviette and shreds it or folds it into shapes, or uses as a paper plane

Shagging

* Air-Shagging items such as their car, chair, walls or anything that gives them a thrill; also known as dry-humping

Shirts

* Always wears lucky shirt
* Clutches at a shirt

Shoes

* Wears different shoes on purpose to see if other people notice

Shopping

* Addicted to shopping sprees
* Calculates the total of items put in a shopping cart and tallies it up in their head

Shrugging

* Shrugs all the time
* Shrugs for no reason

Shyness

* Hides from everybody through shyness

Sickness

* Constantly coughs up phlegm, even when not sick

Silence

* Thinks best in complete silence
* Thinks best with music on

Sings

* Breaks into song unexpectedly
* Forgets the words and makes them up
* Likes to yodel in the privacy of their own home
* Loudly
* Repetitively
* Sings songs despite singing the wrong words or singing out of tune
* Tunelessly
* Under breath

Sky

  * Avoids eye contact – before answering a question looks up to the sky
  * Regularly looks up at the sky to check the position of the sun or moon

Sleeping

  * Always has to sleep with the lights, radio and television on
  * Always has to sleep with a pet if partner is not home
  * Checks that all the doors are locked before going to sleep
  * Falls asleep reading in bed / on public transport

Sliding

  * Slides bangles or bracelets up and down arm
  * Slides the tip of index fingernail up and down along the side of the thumb beside it, especially if there is a snag or nail chip, and plays with it
  * Slides thumbnail along top or bottom row of teeth

Smells

  * Always sprays air freshener about
  * Always wears strong perfume
  * Has significant body odour and doesn't seem to notice
  * Constantly complains about bad smells
  * Farts in hand and 'catches' the smell, then with cupped hand goes to an unsuspecting victim and tells them to 'smell this'
  * House always smells of delicious cooking
  * House always smells of fresh flowers
  * House always smells of freshly baked bread
  * House always smells of freshly brewed coffee
  * Smells the fresh juice of a crushed leaf

Smoking

* Always 'borrows a fag,' never has own
* Addicted to smoking
* Bites people's heads off after quitting smoking
* Eats too much after stopping smoking
* Only smokes socially
* Suffers from smoker's cough

Snapping

* Snaps fingers
* Snaps at people when has given up smoking/caffeine etc.

Sneezing/Sniffing

* Always says 'Bless you' when somebody sneezes
* Has a constant cold
* Sneezes from the slightest dust
* Sniffs glue

Snoring

* Finds it really hard to cope with certain noises, such as snoring

Socks

* Always wears lucky socks
* Wears different socks on purpose to see if other people notice
* Wears only new socks

Songs

* Air drums to songs, real or imaginary
* Driven mad by same song going through mind all the time
* Breaks into song unexpectedly
* Changes radio stations after every song

Sorry

* Always says sorry, even when there's no need or it was somebody else's fault
* Finds it incredibly difficult to say sorry, will try and avoid saying it where possible

Speaking

* Always vocal in public, has to speak the loudest to keep the attention on themselves
* Constantly rubs tummy and says 'Lovely jubbly'
* Excessively uses initials or acronyms for common AND uncommon phrases, never bothers to explain them
* Fails to finish sentences due to anxiety
* Gestures wildly while speaking
* Has a 'Mrs Malaprop' tendency and no amount of polite corrections have an impact. 'Audacity' is always 'adocity'; 'ca ne fait rien' is always 'san fairy anne' or 'purport' is always 'preport'
* Has the ability to speak in a cartoon-like voice which sounds little or nothing like real voice
* Mimics an adult with a deep voice
* Mimics others' voices or accents
* Often finishes other people's sentences
* Repeats the last few words of another person's sentence in a conversation
* Says 'hello' to everyone in the street (and spooks some people by doing this)
* Speaks in a foreign language to exclude somebody
* Speaks in a variety of accents

* Speaks through the corner of the mouth, either under stress or when lying
* Speaks too loudly, over everybody else
* Speaks too quietly
* Speaks while chewing on the side of cheek
* Speaks with mouth full of food or gum
* Speaks in a zany manner with zany body language
* Tends to get lost in thought while people are speaking to them and needs to ask them to repeat themselves

Spectacles

* Constantly cleans the lenses
* Fiddles with them whilst wearing them
* Looks over reading glasses when talking to somebody
* Plays with them
* Pushes up and down nose
* Sucks the end of the arm
* Takes them off and twirls them round
* Uses one pair of glasses for watching cricket and another for watching rugby

Spitting

* Breaks up tiny pieces of napkin and spits it into a straw. Shoots it at unsuspecting people but quickly turns away so the 'shot' person doesn't know who did it

Squinting

* Squints intensely at something because of poor eyesight
* Squints intensely at something out of frustration
* Squints intensely at something through habit

Stamps

* Always sends handwritten letters with carefully chosen stamps. First, they buy philatelic editions from their local post office. Second, they make a point of properly 'theming' a letter to the person they are writes to; for instance, if they know the letter recipient likes cats or Star Wars or they have a special big birthday or they are Royalist, they will choose personality matches stamps. Third, they match the colours of the stamp with the inked address, so the whole thing comes out quite a 'feast for the eye' which always gets them a lot of praise from the letter recipients

Standing

* Always stands with their hands behind their back, sometimes in an 'at ease' position, even though they were never in the military
* Bounces instead of standing still
* Pretends to kick a ball while standing in a group
* Stands and observes instead of getting into the action
* Stands next to somebody at the urinal despite there being space further away

Stealing

* Steals salt and pepper pots from restaurants

Stories

* Compulsively interrupts people telling stories to interject facts that one only knows because one has been told the story before, not because one was involved with it
* Eavesdrops in public, especially restaurants, and makes up stories about the relationships of the people around them

* Has a twitch where they wriggle their nose, especially when telling a long story with lots of detail
* Invents plot scenarios from part personal experience and part make believe for futuristic tales

Strangers

* Raises hand to wave at strangers for a chuckle

Straw

* Breaks up tiny pieces of napkin and spits it into a straw. Shoots it at unsuspecting people but quickly turns away so the 'shot' person doesn't know who did it
* Has to drink everything with a straw

Street

* Always looks both ways before crossing the street
* Says 'hello' to everyone in the street (and spooks some people by doing this)

Stroking

* Stroking long ear hairs

Sucking

* Constantly sucks on the ends of glasses
* Eats a sweet and chews it, doesn't suck it
* Jiggles bottom lip so there is a sucking sound coming from mouth
* Sucks on a cabbage core
* Sucks on hair
* Sucks on a match stick

Sugar

* Has an addiction to sugar and all sweet things
* Hides sugar addiction from people

Sun

* Regularly looks up at the sky to check the position of the sun
* Uses the sun to tell the time

Superstitious

* Carries a lucky charm

Swearing

* Swears as part of everyday conversation
* Swears self-consciously when uncomfortable

Sweating

* Breaks out in a sweat on brow, on nose or under arms either when under pressure or for no apparent reason
* Profusely sweats even when at rest or not worried about anything

Sweets

* Eats a sweet and chews it, doesn't suck it
* Eats sweets and straightens out the wrappers or makes something from them
* Folds sweet wrapper into tiny nob and tosses it around the room, fidgeting with it or sticking it into something

Switching

* Always switches lights off when leaving a room; complains if others do not do it
* Switches kettle off just before it boils

* Switches the light on and off twice before either entering or
  leaving the room
* Switches the oven off halfway through cooking
* Switches the toaster off just before toast is ready

T

Table

* Constantly jiggles leg, often at a table, when nervous or bored; then when leg is exhausted moves to other leg
* Has to have all papers or books on a table in perfect order, all stacked up and square with no papers sticking out; if any become out of line or messed up, squares them again
* Moves things around the table
* Puts feet on a desk or table
* When dining out, always tidies up the table and resets the condiments

Talking

* Constantly rubs tummy and says 'Lovely jubbly'
* Excessively uses initials or acronyms for common AND uncommon phrases, never bothers to explain them
* Fails to finish sentences due to anxiety

* Gesticulates wildly with hands
* Has a 'Mrs Malaprop' tendency and no amount of polite corrections have an impact. 'Audacity' is always 'adocity'; 'ca ne fait rien' is always 'san fairy anne,' and 'purport' is always 'preport'
* Has the ability to speak in a cartoon-like voice which sounds little or nothing like real voice
* Mimics an adult with a deep voice
* Mimics others' voices or accents
* Often finishes other people's sentences
* Talks quietly, making everybody strain to hear
* Repeats the last few words of the other person's sentence in a conversation
* Says hello cheerfully to everyone passing by
* Stutters when meeting new people and then talks normally afterwards
* Talks to oneself, an internal monologue
* Talks about oneself in the third person
* Talks with mouth full of food or gum
* Talks with hands

Tapping

* Always taps someone's arm and says something like 'Hey, get a load of this.'
* Knife and fork like musical instruments
* Fingers/a pen on the table
* Nose
* Repetitively taps somebody's arm without noticing
* Taps a foot without any music being heard

Tea

  * Always has a cup of tea on the go
  * Unable to go an hour without a cup of tea, even when travelling – but then must have constant trips to the loo
  * Obsessive that tea is correct shade of brown, even uses paint chart to check
  * Takes own tea abroad

Technology

  * Addicted to checking emails
  * Addicted to checking text messages
  * Always opens emails as they come in
  * Always looks at phone, even when in company
  * Always surfs the net
  * Keeps computer/laptop running in the background at all times
  * Never starts or ends the day without checking emails

Teeth

  * Clacks them together
  * Grinds jaw or teeth, sometimes self-consciously (teeth have actually cracked and broken because of this. Most commonly, the face muscles really ache and headaches result)
  * Grinds teeth at night or in the day, or when bored
  * Picks at teeth in public
  * Picks food out with toothpick or fingernail
  * Runs tongue over front teeth
  * Slides thumb nail along top or bottom row of teeth
  * Taps fingernail against them
  * Uses someone else's toothbrush. Other character is either shocked or doesn't know

Television

* Always has to sleep with the television on
* Leaves the television on during the day for the pets to have 'someone' home
* Watches *The Sound of Music* constantly, just to practise yodelling along to 'The Lonely Goatherd'

Thinking

* Has a tendency to get lost in thought while people are speaking and needs to ask them to repeat themselves
* Submits to the ideas and suggestions of others without thinking of one's own needs
* Thinks best in complete silence
* Thinks best with music on
* Thinks hard before saying yes to requests, even if as sim-ple as 'Would you like a cup of tea?'
* When thinking, walks past a row of hedges, yanks off a green leaf and crumbles it up in their hand because they like the crunchy feeling as the leaf breaks up into little pieces. Smelling the fresh juice of the leaf as it gets on their hand makes them think of spring and connects them to nature

Thriftiness

* Always looks out for a bargain
* Saving electricity
  - Leaves the lights off and snoops around in the dark
  - Switches the kettle off just before it boils
  - Switches the toaster off just before toast is done
* Saving gas

- Leaves the oven door open to heat the kitchen
- Switches the oven off halfway through cooking

* Saving water
  - Does not flush the loo each time
  - Only showers every other day

* Thrifty nearly to the point of being obsessive or compulsive

Thumbs

* Absentmindedly spins pen or pencil across the top of the thumbnail
* Constantly sticks thumb in eye socket
* Slides the tip of index fingernail up and down along the side of the thumb beside it, especially if there is a snag or nail chip, and plays with it
* Slides thumbnail along top or bottom row of teeth
* Thumbs nose like a violin

Ties

* Collects ties; even owning 100s, still must collect more, despite never wearing any
* Only wears a tie if they belong to the organisation it represents

Time

* Adopts silly or cartoon-like voices in times of nervousness or stress
* Always early, makes sure to arrive for a meeting at least fifteen minutes early. If it's a speaking event, arrives an hour early ('fess up time, this is me!)
* Always knows the directions, even if visiting a city for the first time
* Always late, this person lives on the edge of time, never gets stressed when late ('fess up time, this is my husband!)

* Driven mad by same song going through mind all the time
* Checks how somebody is throughout time together
* Dusts all the time
* Extends leg each time they sit down
* Has to style moustache/hair exactly every time
* Keeps computer/laptop running in the background at all times
* Quotes movies/television shows all the time
* Does not flush the loo each time
* Practises keepy-uppy all the time
  (bounces a ball on their knee or foot to keep it up off the floor)
* Sneaks back to the kitchen, time after time, to snack on
  more chocolate
* Spends hours each day painting toenails
* Spends time watching people going by and making up stories
  about their lives
* Unable to sit still at any time
* Uses the sun to tell the time
* Washes hands at least three times after uses a public bathroom,
  even at one's friends' or family's home
* Wears a pen or pencil behind the ear at all times

Toaster

* Switches the toaster off just before toast is ready to save electricity

Toes

* Cracks toes by bending them right over until hearing them crack
* Likes the feeling of bare toes on the floor/ground
* Lets toenails grow extra long
* Paints toenails different colours to suit sandals/outfits

* Picks at toes constantly until they are a mess

* Picks toenails

* Spends hours each day painting toenails

* Wriggles toes deep into sand

Toilet Habits

* Unable to go an hour without a cup of tea, even when travelling –
  but then must have constant trips to the loo

* Compelled to wash a glass before drinking from it, even in a
  restaurant, so must take a trip to the loo before having a drink

* Drips water over the floor

* Forgets to flush

* Has to have double thick toilet paper or won't wee

* Has to have the loo roll facing down, not over the top

* Leaves cubicle door open

* Misses the toilet/urinal and pees on floor/shoes

* Does not flush loo each time

* Does not wash hands

* Only able to pee if public toilet is empty

* Only uses cubicle, never urinal

* Pees in circles around the bowl

* Pees up the wall to see if it can be done in a straight line

* Stands next to somebody at the urinal despite there being space
  further away

* Uses toilet seat covers and never touches the handle

* Washes hands over and over again

Toothbrush

* Uses someone else's toothbrush. Other character is either shocked or doesn't know

Toothpaste

* Never puts the toothpaste lid back on after use
* Squeezes toothpaste in the middle

Toothpicks

* Plays with toothpicks, makes shapes with them or makes a pile and crashes it

Trousers

* Always walks with hands in pockets
* Excessively rearranges when sitting down
* Plays with balls (the testicular type) and fiddles or jostles them around in their hands, even in public; can often be doing this with their hands buried in their trousers while having a conversation
* Scratches ass to the extent that it causes the trouser leg to ride up and down
* Wears them too high up on waist
* Wears them too low down, around backside

Tugging

* Tugs at ears or earrings

Tummy

* Constantly rubs tummy and says 'Lovely jubbly'

Tunes

* Whistles out of tune
* Whistles strange tunes

Twirling

* Constantly twirls necklace between fingers
* Takes glasses off and twirls them
* Twirls hair into shapes, lets it spring back and then starts all over again
* Twirls hair and then sucks on it

Twitching

* Has a twitch where they wiggle their nose, especially when telling a long story with lots of detail
* Mouth
* Raises eyebrows for no reason while speaking, either purposely or accidentally as a twitch
* Twitches certain parts of the body for no apparent reason
* When nervous

U

Uncrossing Legs

　* Crosses and uncrosses legs, when nervous, bored or agitated about something

Using

　* Excessively uses initials or acronyms for common AND uncommon phrases, never bothers to explain them

　* Uses someone else's toothbrush. Other character is either shocked or doesn't know

V

View

* Regularly sits on a beach and looks toward the horizon to clear their head with a minimal, uncluttered view

Violin

* Thumbs nose like a violin

Visiting

* Always knows directions, even if visiting a city for the first time
* So into nature that when they feel like being naked they take clothes off, no matter who is visiting

Vocal

* Always vocal in public, has to speak the loudest to keep the attention on themselves

Voice

* Can have a high pitched voice, depending on mood
* Can have a low, raspy voice, depending on mood

* Has the ability to speak in a cartoon-like voice which sounds little or nothing like real voice
* Mimics an adult with a deep voice
* Mimics others' voices or accents

W

Walking

* Always drags feet while walking
* Always walks with hands in pockets
* Likes to walk in a zig zag pattern, rather than a straight line
* Walks in the middle of any aisle or pavement, forcing other people to move aside or around one
* Walks into things while reading

Washing

* Allows dishes to pile up and go unwashed for days
* Feels compelled to wash a glass before drinking from it, even in a restaurant, so must take a trip to the loo before having a drink
* Forgets to wash hands
* Never washes dishes
* Places dirty dishes on top of one another in the sink
* Obsessively washes hands/dishes
* Spends hours in the bath/bathroom
* Wipes the counter again and again

Watch

* Always wears a watch, panics if forgets to put it on
* Constantly glances at watch to check time
* Never wears a watch, has an innate sense of time

Water

* Always takes a hot bath; not just hot, scorching hot. If water is lukewarm or mildly hot will not get in ('fess up time, this is me!)
* Unable to go to bed without a full glass of water, but seldom drinks any of it
* Chews caps of water bottles
* Saves water
* Does not flush toilet every time
* Only showers every other day

Waving

* Raises hand to wave at strangers for a chuckle
* Raises hand to wave at strangers for no apparent reason

Weakness

* Has a weakness for rescuing stray animals

Wearing

* Always wears lucky hat, socks, shirt or other article of clothing
* Collects ties; even owning 100s still must collect more, despite never wearing any
* Only wears a tie if they belong to the organisation it represents
* Plays with holes in ears, even when not wearing earrings
* Wears baseball cap back to front
* Wears different socks or shoes on purpose to see if people notice
* Wears only new socks

Whistling

* Constantly
* Happily
* Loudly
* Repetitively
* Whistles out of tune
* Whistles strange tunes

Winking

* Constantly calls someone 'luv' and gives them a forced wink
* Winks as a form of flirting
* Winks as a twitch
* Winks on purpose for fun

Wiping

* Wipes the counter again and again

Worry

* Profusely sweats even when at rest and not worried about anything

Wrappers

* Eats sweets and straightens out the wrappers or makes something from them
* Folds sweet wrapper into tiny nob and tosses it around the room, fidgeting with it or sticking it into something

Wriggling

* Wriggles eyebrows

Wringing

* Constantly wrings hands or particular fingers, sometimes behind back

Writing

* Always dots i's with a smiley face or heart

* Always scribbles ideas down

* Always sends stories to magazines/newspapers in the hope of publication

* Carries a notebook at all times

* Starts writing novels but never finishes them

* Writes phrases and ideas on index cards to use them later in fiction

* Writes with left hand but does everything else right-handed

X

Xenophobia

* Has a fear of foreigners
* Has a huge dislike of people from a different country

X-rays

* Always tries to sneak a look at any x-rays on display when visiting a hospital
* Pretends they have x-ray vision by telling everyone they can see what they're doing

Xerodermia

* Suffers from abnormal dryness of the skin and always picks and scratches at dry bits of skin

Xerostomia

* Has excessive dryness of the mouth and always licks lips to try and wet mouth, or chews gum to wet palate

Xylophagous

*Always chews on bits of wood

Xylophone

* Always plays with xylophone or runs fingers across it to hear the sound

X-treme

*Participates in x-treme sports to get a buzz

Y

Yawning

* Can't seem to stop yawning, even when not tired

* Opens mouth ridiculously wide when yawning

* Yawns the moment they see somebody else yawning

Yearning

*Always yearns to be somewhere else

* Has an unrequited yearning for a work colleague

*Always yearns for more in life

Yelling

* Always yells at people out of anger

* Yells when excited

Yes

* Always says yes to every request, even if it puts them out

* Acts as a yes-man or yes-woman with a 'yes, yes, yes' in every
  other sentence

* Thinks hard before saying yes to requests, even if as simple as 'Would you like a cup of tea?'

Yodelling

* Likes to yodel in the privacy of their own home
* Watches *The Sound of Music* constantly, just to practise yodelling along to 'The Lonely Goatherd'

Yoga

* Finds peace when meditating through yoga
* Dresses for yoga and has all the equipment but never ac-tually does it

Yoghurts

* Always keeps the fridge full of fat-free yoghurts as part of a never-ending diet
* Eats yoghurts after every meal

Youthful

* Always on a quest to make themselves look ever more youthful

Z

Zany

* Has a very zany sense of humour

* Finds zaniness hard to put up with

* Speaks in a zany manner with zany body language

Zest

* Has a real zest for life

Zealous

*Always zealous about any tasks given to them

* Always devoted to a greater cause

Zips

* Often absentmindedly forgets to zip up

* Prefers zips to buttons on clothes

Zig Zag

* Likes to walk in a zig zag pattern, rather than a straight line

Zits

* Makes a colossal fuss whenever even the smallest spot appears
* Suffers from bad zits, has scars on face

Zombies

* Always dresses as a zombie for fancy dress parties
* Obsessed with watching films about zombies

The End
of
A~Z Writers' Character Quirks

If you enjoyed reading *A~Z of Writers' Character Quirks,* please take a moment to share your thoughts with a review Amazon, Goodreads, Kobo, iBooks or Smashwords. It doesn't have to be glowing, only genuine and fair. All you need to do is click the review link on this book's page. Thank you for your support!

Writers' Resource Series

Powerful Writing Produces Bestsellers: Secrets of How to Write a Novel Using Techniques from the Best Reference Guides on Creative Writing

&

A~Z Writers' Character Quirks: Writers' A~ Z of Behaviours, Foibles, Habits, Mannerisms & Quirks for Writers to Create Fictional Characters

&

101 Writers' Scene Settings: Unique Location Ideas & Sensory Details for Writers to Create Vivid Scene Settings
Check for future editions: http://paulawynne.com/writers-resource-series

Bonus material

1. Don't forget to pick up your FREE copy of *Pimp My Fiction* here:
   http://eepurl.com/bC336f

2. Join Paula Wynne's mailing list to receive the latest news about upcoming releases and specials just for subscribers:
   http://eepurl.com/byjPVT

If you stay on Paula's mailing list, you will be given the opportunity to get a free review copy of her next books.

3. Scenes Checklist: Download Paula's Scenes Checklist to create your scenes:
   http://eepurl.com/bC_vjX

4. Settings Checklist: Download Paula's Settings Checklist with sensory details for writers' to create vivid scene settings:
   http://eepurl.com/bC_vjX

5. Free sample chapters of *Pimp My Site*
   http://eepurl.com/byv2wT

6. Free sample chapters of *The Grotto's Secret*:
   http://eepurl.com/bCahBf

Acknowledgments

Thank you to friends and family who contributed their habits and quirks. And, without them knowing, the wonderful range of people I have secretly watched over the years. Thank you to the following contributors who didn't mind their names being listed in a 'quirky' book: Sharon Bassett, Jane Cable, Lisa Devaney, Adele Friedman, Susanne More, Kent Wynne.

A big thanks to Rosalind Brookman who always gives me excellent feedback and advice. Ros helped me set out and organise the A~Z to make it easier for writers to find the quirks quickly.

About The Author

As an award-winning entrepreneur Paula Wynne has appeared on TV several times, including breakfast shows and has been featured in various magazines and national newspapers.

Paula and her husband Ken starred in the BBC Show, *Escape to the Continent*, which showed their quest to live in Spain so Paula could become a full time writer.

For many years Paula has been obsessed with learning everything to improve her writing. She has acquired a bookshelf of excellent reference books by highly acclaimed authors, so she wrote *Pimp My Fiction*: Secrets of How to Write a Novel. This inspired a Writers' Resource Series with *101 Writers' Scene Settings* and *A~Z Writers' Character Quirks*.

Paula received an 'Honourable Mention' in the 75th Annual Writers Digest Writing Competition for two unpublished novels.

Now Paula is really excited to be publishing her first novel, *The Grotto's Secret*.

9 781530 622023